The MacGregors And MacDougalls

Written by Quentin Flynn
Illustrated by Ian Forss

Contents	Page
Chapter 1. *A worm sandwich!*	4
Chapter 2. *A family feud*	9
Chapter 3. *Footballs and Venn diagrams*	15
Chapter 4. *The strangest thing*	20
Chapter 5. *A surprising award*	24
Chapter 6. *Some things never change*	27
Verse	32

The MacGregors And MacDougalls

With these characters . . .

Griffin
MacGregor

Des
MacDougall

Gerry
MacGregor

Ivan
Inverness

Douglas
MacDougall

"It had all begun

Setting the scene . . .

For three hundred long years, the MacGregor family and the MacDougall family have been arguing. It all started because a wall was accidentally built in the wrong place, and ever since then, fathers and sons from both families have been behaving badly!

When Ivan Inverness, the principal of Killarnoch School, decides that the arguing must stop, he decides to try an unusual punishment to make the two youngest members of the families work together. Even Ivan doesn't think that his scheme will work—but there are surprising results in store for the MacGregors and the MacDougalls!

one foggy morning in 1699 ..."

Chapter 1.

Ivan Inverness, the principal of Killarnoch Elementary School, paced up and down behind his desk. His bushy white eyebrows curved down and met in the middle of his forehead as he thought about the problem he faced.

Behind Ivan Inverness the walls were covered with old photographs of all the classes that had been at Killarnoch Elementary School for the last hundred years. His desk was piled high with papers, books, and letters. His eyes settled on two nervous students staring at the floor and fidgeting in front of his desk.

"Once more, you are in deep trouble, Griffin MacGregor," growled Ivan Inverness. Griffin, the smaller of the two boys, squirmed in his chair. The other boy nudged him in the ribs and made a face until the principal spoke to him as well. "And don't think that you will get away with this either, Des MacDougall."

Ivan Inverness's eyebrows moved like a long, hairy caterpillar as he spoke firmly. "You are *both* in deep trouble."

"But it was that sneak Griffin who *put* the worm in my sandwich!" protested Des in a voice as big and rough as he looked. "He started it, so *he* should be punished."

"Don't interrupt! It was *you* who forced Griffin to *eat* the sandwich," replied the principal grimly.

Griffin bit his bottom lip and grimaced as he remembered the taste of the worm. Des put his hands over his mouth to hide a big smirk.

Ivan Inverness sighed. Ever since he had been at Killarnoch Elementary School, this had been a recurring problem. The MacGregors and the MacDougalls simply could not get along. He stared at an old photograph from 1965 and focused on the young faces of the boys' fathers, Gerry MacGregor and Douglas MacDougall. In 1965, Ivan's first year as principal of Killarnoch, both Gerry and Douglas looked exactly like their sons. Ivan sighed again.

Even the boys' fathers had fought at school, he remembered. Just as the boys' grandfathers had fought, too, when Ivan was a boy in their class. In fact, it had been the same problem for three hundred years.

Ivan Inverness folded his arms, having finally thought of a punishment.

"Griffin, you will help Des with his homework for a week. Des, you will help Griffin with his soccer practice for a week. That way, you may learn that each of you has different strengths, and that you should use them to help each other, not to hurt each other."

Ivan Inverness secretly thought it was highly unlikely that the two boys would learn *anything*, but it was the best solution he could think of. There was only one quarter left of the school year, and then both Des and Griffin would leave for high school. He might get some peace at his school during the last quarter—but he wouldn't be surprised if there was no peace between the MacGregors and the MacDougalls for another three hundred years.

The boys glared at each other.

"It's not fair," they both complained.

"Well, I'm glad you agree on at least *one* thing," retorted their principal. "Now hurry back to class. And behave yourselves!"

Chapter 2.

"You hid a worm in Des MacDougall's sandwich?" chuckled Griffin MacGregor's father, Gerry. "That's my good boy," he said, beaming proudly. "Well done!"

"Don't encourage him," warned his mother, Emily. "You should be setting an example by ending the feud between our families."

"You're right, hon," said Gerry. He turned back to his son. "Did I ever tell you about the time I hid a mouse in Douglas MacDougall's lunch box? Now, that was a sight to see! That big, hairy oaf almost fell off his chair when the mouse leapt out at him at lunchtime! Ha ha ha!"

Griffin listened intently as his father told him all the hilarious tricks he had played on his enemy when he was at school. Emily MacGregor decided to ignore her husband and noisily turned the pages of her newspaper. She could still hear the usual words, however, such as "prank", "beetle milkshake" and "dumb-dumb."

Over at the MacDougall house, Douglas MacDougall was clapping his son on the shoulder.

"Excellent, my boy," he was saying loudly. "Forcing that MacGregor boy to eat a worm sandwich? This boy's turning out to be a real MacDougall!"

"Oh, Douglas, do shut up!" said his wife, Hettie, angrily.

"Did I ever tell you about the time I forced Gerry MacGregor to eat a whole box of plums one lunchtime? He was sick for the next three days!" Douglas MacDougall's moustache waggled as he roared with laughter. He was delighted that his son was keeping the family feud alive.

The families' feuding had begun one foggy morning in 1699. Des MacDougall's great-great-great-great-grandpa, Larry MacDougall, was carefully pegging out a string line. He was building a new stone wall along the border of his land and the MacGregor farm.

Thomas and Gracie MacGregor and Doris MacDougall went out in the evening to see Larry's work.

"Looks good to me," raved Thomas.

"My sons and I will start building tomorrow," Larry replied.

That night, while the families slept, one of Thomas MacGregor's goats, Milly, wandered from her pen. She found Larry's left-over lunch by a raspberry bush beside the wall-to-be. She ate it in one gulp.

On her way home, Milly snagged her leg on the string line. She pulled the line back and forth until she untangled herself. But the MacDougall farm increased in size by the length of one goat after Milly had pulled the string this way and that.

The next morning, the muscular MacDougalls worked hard to stack the stones to fit perfectly along the line of the string. They worked for weeks. Thomas and Gracie watched from their upstairs window as the wall took shape.

At last, when the wall was finished, both families met for a picnic.

As he sat admiring the wall, Thomas noticed something odd. The raspberry bush that was usually on his farm now stood on the other side of the wall. Of course, no one knew about Milly's night-time wandering, and so the feud began.

Thomas MacGregor accused the MacDougalls of deliberately stealing his land. "You cheat, MacDougall!" he shouted.

Larry MacDougall was terribly offended. "You could have helped build the wall, you puny wimp!" he yelled back.

The two families would not talk to each other from that day on. That is, until Ivan Inverness intervened ...

Chapter 3.

The next day, Griffin MacGregor trudged out to the soccer field. He always felt he was too small to play soccer well. And he *especially* didn't like the idea of soccer practice with Des MacDougall. At the other end of the field stood Des, kicking the ball with an evil smirk on his face.

"Come on, Griffin," yelled Des impatiently. He wheeled around and kicked the ball ferociously into the goal. The net stretched with the force of Des's shot.

When the ball rolled back to Des, he kicked the ball straight at Griffin.

Thump! The ball hit Griffin right in the chest and nearly knocked him over. Des ran up to him and dribbled the ball around and around Griffin before kicking it at him again. Thump! This time, it hit Griffin on the shoulder.

"Kick it back, you wimpy MacGregor," yelled Des. He kicked it again, and Griffin tried to duck. Now Griffin was becoming angry. This was not fair! After all, *he* was the one who had been forced to eat the worm sandwich. And now he would be black and blue all over with bruises from the soccer ball.

"Like this?" asked Griffin. "I'll get you back *harder*," he thought angrily. He put all his might into a huge kick aimed straight at his enemy.

The ball curved around Des at high speed and slammed into the goal. Des MacDougall looked surprised.

"Lucky shot," he sulked, as he fetched the ball. "Bet you can't do that again!"

Griffin was furious. He wanted to kick the ball straight at Des's head. But he missed again, and the ball whistled past Des MacDougall's left ear and thumped into the goal.

Des didn't say anything, but he looked amazed. He dribbled the ball up to Griffin, and tried to get past him. But Griffin was smaller and faster, and flicked the ball out from underneath Des's feet. Des pushed him out of the way and took the ball back. He spun around and was about to shoot for goal himself, just to show this MacGregor how easy it was.

But Griffin stood in the way and the ball bounced off his head.

Des was about to laugh until he saw where the ball had bounced. It rolled into the goal.

"Wow," he whispered. "That was a good header!"

After school, both boys had to stay behind for an hour so that Griffin could help Des with his math homework.

Des stared at the graph paper in front of him. His eyes glazed over. He hated math. He didn't understand it at all. Anyway, what use was math going to be?

They were studying sets and Venn diagrams.

"It's easy," said Griffin, sighing and rolling his eyes. Des looked at the two sets in front of him. Numbers surrounded by circles. What was that supposed to mean?

"Think of them as two groups of people. This can be your family," said Griffin, pointing at one set of numbers. "And this can be my family," he said, pointing at the other.

Then he drew the two circles so they overlapped. There were two numbers in the part where both circles overlapped.

"These two numbers are in both circles. Think of them as the only MacGregor and the only MacDougall to talk to each other," explained Griffin.

Des chewed on the end of his pencil. He was puzzled.

"But no one in our families talks to each other," he said.

"We do," said Griffin. Slowly, Des stopped chewing his pencil.

"So," he said hesitantly, "these are the sneaky numbers and these are the strong numbers?"

Griffin sighed and flopped back in his chair. Des was on the right track, but this was going to be a long hour!

Ivan Inverness, the principal, peered in through the classroom window. His caterpillar eyebrows curled as he saw the two boys huddled together.

"Well, well," he said to himself. "I never thought I'd see the day when a MacGregor and a MacDougall would work together without a fight."

Chapter 4.

At the cannery where the boys' fathers worked, machinery hissed and clattered as cans of salmon were filled and sealed. Gerry MacGregor stood at one end of the factory line and Douglas MacDougall stood at the other. They never spoke to each other.

Gerry MacGregor turned to the factory worker next to him and nudged her.

"My boy Griffin is teaching that great hairy oaf's boy to do math," he said, sneering. "Have you ever heard anything so ridiculous?"

Douglas MacDougall looked up and glared at Gerry MacGregor.

"Those MacDougalls are so dumb they have to count all their fingers at the end of the day to remind themselves how many toes they have!" Gerry continued. "And even then, they have to do it twice to make sure they're right."
He giggled.

Douglas MacDougall turned to the factory worker next to him.

"My boy Des is teaching that little sneak's boy to play soccer," he said and guffawed. "Can you imagine that?"

Gerry MacGregor narrowed his eyes at Douglas MacDougall.

"The last time a MacGregor played soccer," snorted Douglas, "we used him *as* the soccer ball! Even then, he was useless. He didn't bounce very well at all!" Douglas laughed loudly and pretended to kick an imaginary MacGregor around the floor.

However, amazingly, after a week, both Des and Griffin were looking forward to math homework and soccer practice.

"Let's start with triangles, rectangles and parallelograms," suggested Griffin. Des eagerly brought out his graph paper and drew a perfect set of shapes.

"That was easy," he said proudly. "Let's move on to some harder stuff."

After an hour of homework, Des showed Griffin how to kick the soccer ball backward over his head. Griffin flicked the ball up into the air and kicked a perfect goal over his head.

"Goal!" yelled Des excitedly. "Now try this shot." He showed Griffin a slide kick.

Ivan Inverness was amazed to see that even though the punishment week was over, the boys still practiced soccer and did their homework together. He smiled to himself as he peered out his window and saw Griffin and Des dribbling a soccer ball around and around each other.

"This really is the strangest thing," he said, shaking his head. "Who would have ever thought?"

Chapter 5.

At the end of the school year, there was a big awards ceremony at Killarnoch Elementary School. The parents and friends arrived and sat in the school hall. There was a murmur in the crowd as Ivan Inverness strode onto the stage.

"I'd like to welcome you all to the Killarnoch Millennium Awards Ceremony," he said proudly. "We will start the awarding of prizes. And then, we have a few surprises planned."

Everyone looked at each other. What did Mr. Inverness mean?

Ivan read out the list of prizewinners. First, he named the winner of the English prize, followed by the winner of the arts prize. Then, he read out the winner of the social studies prize. All the students collected their prizes to the sound of people clapping enthusiastically.

At the end of the ceremony, Ivan raised his hands for silence.

"And now," he said, beaming, "we have two special prizes."

"For the most improved math student," he said, looking around the hall. "The prize goes to ..."

Gerry MacGregor nudged his wife, Emily. "It'll be Griffin, for sure," he said, sitting up proudly, and getting ready to clap.

Ivan looked at his notes.

"Des MacDougall!"

There was a shocked silence in the hall. No one looked more shocked than Gerry MacGregor. Except, perhaps, Douglas MacDougall. He stared at his wife, Hettie.

"Did I hear right? A math prize?"

But Hettie just stood up and cheered. Everyone else in the hall stood up, too, and started to clap loudly. Des MacDougall walked proudly on stage, and waved at the crowd. Ivan handed him the prize, a new compass, and then he cleared his throat.

"Ahem," he said. "And now for the other special prize of the evening—the most improved athlete."

Douglas MacDougall sat up straight. "Des is about to get two prizes," he whispered excitedly to Hettie. "That'll annoy those sneaky MacGregors."

"Griffin MacGregor!" shouted Ivan Inverness.

Gerry MacGregor's mouth dropped open. He stared at his wife, but Emily was already on her feet, clapping and cheering. "Go, Griffin!" she yelled. The people clapped and cheered wildly.

Griffin walked proudly onto the stage and collected his prize, a pair of soccer socks. Then he walked over to where Des was standing and shook his hand. Everyone clapped and cheered even louder. In three hundred years, no one had seen anything like it. This was unbelievable—but true! A MacDougall had won a math prize—and a MacGregor had won a sports prize!

Chapter 6.

The next morning, the factory workers were talking about the awards ceremony. They couldn't wait until Gerry and Douglas arrived at work.

Both men strolled in looking very pleased with themselves. But instead of standing at opposite ends of the canning line Gerry walked up to Douglas and gave him a nudge.

The other workers stopped. The machines hissed and clattered to a stop. Was there going to be a fight? Instead, Gerry smiled at Douglas.

"That was very nice of your boy to help Griffin," said Gerry to Douglas. "He's the first MacGregor to ever win a prize for sports. Old Ivan Inverness thinks he'll go on to play for the national team one day," said Gerry proudly.

Douglas smiled back at Gerry.

"Well, Hettie and I were grateful that your boy helped Des," he said gruffly. "We've never had a math prizewinner in our family. Inverness says if Des keeps studying, he'll earn a scholarship to the university."

Everyone at the factory stared as the two men settled down to work side by side. No one could ever remember a MacGregor and a MacDougall working side by side before—not in a hundred years of canning salmon in Killarnoch.

Even more amazing was that Douglas MacDougall sat down next to Gerry MacGregor during the lunch break. The lunch room fell silent as the other factory workers wondered what would happen next. This was a most peculiar day.

"Maybe it's time we stopped fighting," said Douglas, leaning over to Gerry.

"Maybe," agreed Gerry. There was an awkward silence for a few seconds. Then Gerry spoke again.

"Would you like to share a sandwich?"

No one in the lunch room was more amazed than Douglas, but he smiled graciously and nodded. Gerry held out his lunch box and flipped open the lid.

Suddenly, the silence in the lunch room was shattered as Douglas MacDougall let out a huge scream and toppled backward off his chair. A tiny gray mouse leapt out of the lunch box and skittered across the floor.

"You great hairy oaf!" laughed Gerry. "At last! I've been wanting to make you fall off your chair for thirty years!"

Douglas MacDougall frowned and started to make a furious face. But as he looked up and saw the tears of laughter rolling down his old enemy's face, he laughed, too. He picked himself off the floor and nudged Gerry in the ribs.

"I'll bring lunch tomorrow," he said, between gasps for air. "I've got a nice box of plums sitting at home, and I remember just how much you like plums."

After three hundred years, the MacGregors and the MacDougalls had finally stopped fighting. And back in his principal's office, Ivan Inverness sat with a smile on his face. He looked up at the newest photograph on his wall—the class of '99. It was the only photograph in sight where a MacGregor and a MacDougall were standing next to each other with big smiles on their faces.

He somehow knew it wouldn't be the last.

"Now, if only I can think of a way to stop the Mazzellis and the MacDonalds from bickering. And the Wangs and the Grabowskis."

He shook his head and smiled. He wondered what the photograph of the class of 2000 would look like.

"One trick more!"

For three hundred years and more,
Two feuding clans have been at war.

One side wiry, one side strong,
Both sides silly, both sides wrong.

There seems no answer to this mess!
Each family bent on more distress!

Then with a principal's persuasion,
Soccer practice and math equations,

Two sons do stop the families' fight,
With surprise results on awards night.

Two fathers, proud and pleased as punch,
Do sit together to share their lunch.

There is, however, a surprise in store …
A final chance for one trick more!